9/03

Explorers & Exploration

The Travels of Lewis & Clark

By Lara Bergen
Illustrated by Patrick O'Brien

Raintree Steck-Vaughn Publishers

A Harcourt Company

Austin · New York
www.steck-vaughn.com

Published by Raintree Steck-Vaughn Publishers, an imprint of Steck-Vaughn Company

Library of Congress Cataloging-in-Publication Data
Bergen, Lara Rice
    Lewis and Clark/by Lara Bergen
        p. cm. — (Explorers and exploration)
    Summary: Describes the expedition led by Meriwether Lewis and William Clark to explore the unknown western regions of America at the beginning of the nineteenth century.
    ISBN 0-7398-1486-9
    1. Lewis and Clark expedition (1804–1806)—Juvenile literature   2. Lewis, Meriwether, 1774–1809—Juvenile literature   3. Clark, William, 1770–1838—Juvenile literature   4. West (U.S.)—Discovery and exploration—Juvenile literature   [1. Lewis and Clark expedition (1804–1806)   2. Lewis, Meriwether, 1774–1809.   3. Clark, William, 1770–1838.   4. West (U.S.)—Discovery and exploration.]
    I. Title. II. Series.

F592.7 B46 2000
917.804'2—dc21   99-055477

Printed in the United States of America
10 9 8 7 6 5 4 3 2 1 LB 03 02 01 00

Produced by By George Productions, Inc.

Ilustration Acknowledgments:
pp. 4, 16, 20, 22, 24, 30–31, 32–33, New York Public Library Picture Collection; p. 7 National Portrait Gallery; p. 29 Reproduced from the Collections of the Library of Congress #13932; p. 40, John Blazejewski. All other artwork is by Patrick O'Brien.

Contents

Lockers, must be 2 – 6 wide &
do – do – – – 31 feet Long ⎬ 156 foot of Plank
do about – – 1 – 6 Deep

Lockers on the Cabin 14 – 0 – long
do – wide 3 – 0 – wide ⎬ 84 feet
do – – – 3 – 0 – Deep

Enos & Robinson do do do   60
                                            ———
                                            300
Calculating for Iron & wood   75
                                            ———
                                            375

a foot too deep to let down of 32 feet log

SETTING OFF

May 21, 1804

On May 21, 1804, a group of adventurers set out from St. Charles, Missouri, to explore the West for the first time.

Native Americans had lived in the West for thousands of years. Since the 1790s, white traders had been sailing around South America to the Pacific coast. But no American colonist had ever traveled across North America. Now, at last, Meriwether Lewis and his partner, William Clark, planned to do just that. In their group were Clark's slave, York, and a crew of more than 40 strong young men. Even a dog—Lewis's Newfoundland, Seaman—was coming along. Two large canoes and one long keelboat would carry them. Lewis called this important expedition the "Corps of Discovery."

The two leaders made many notes and sketches about their journey. This picture shows Clark's sketch of a keelboat.

Until 1803 the United States ended at the Mississippi River. Everything between it and the Pacific Ocean was unexplored. Then President Thomas Jefferson bought about 910,000 square miles (2,350,000 sq km) west of the Mississippi from the French. This "Louisiana Purchase" doubled the size of the country.

For years Jefferson had dreamed of finding a Northwest Passage. Many believed there was an easy way of getting from the east coast to the northwest coast by river. In those days the fastest way to get anywhere was by boat. A Northwest Passage would be safer and faster than sailing around South America. It would give the United States an advantage over England. England already controlled Canada and wanted to control the rest of the Northwest, too. Jefferson knew just the man to lead such an expedition—Meriwether Lewis.

Meriwether Lewis grew up on a Virginia plantation, reading explorers' journals and dreaming of adventure. As a young man, Lewis was an army officer in the wild frontiers of Ohio. Then in 1801 Thomas Jefferson became president of the United States. Before he was even sworn in, Jefferson wrote to Lewis asking him to be his secretary.

The newly built White House was damp and drafty. But Lewis loved living there and working with the president. When Jefferson offered him the chance in 1803 to lead an expedition across the continent, Lewis was excited.

Lewis ordered supplies of all kinds—from guns and ammunition to food and medicine. He had studied with the nation's best scientists. Lewis learned how to navigate, or steer, a boat. He could read and make maps. He could also identify certain plants. He learned about animals and rocks and soil. He even learned how to perform surgery.

A portrait of Thomas Jefferson

Lewis also bought 100 quill pens, ink, and candles so he would be able to write at night. Lewis planned to record as much as possible. He wanted to write about the land, its plants and animals, and the people who lived there.

Lewis knew he would need a partner. So he wrote to a friend from the army, William Clark. Clark had lived most of his life on the frontier, and he was a born leader. The job was perfect for Clark, who agreed to join Lewis.

Together Lewis and Clark spent the fall finding men to serve on their expedition. They looked for men who were strong and not afraid. They looked for men who could live in the wilderness for a year, if not more. Then they spent the winter training them at a camp near the mouth of the Missouri River. By May the entire crew was ready and eager to make history.

The Big Muddy

May 1804–October 1804

For the rest of the spring and summer, the Missouri River was the Corps of Discovery's home. But it was not a comfortable one. The river was called "The Big Muddy" for good reason. It was full of mud, sand, and pieces of wood. And the corps had to travel against the river's current. The hot summer days on the Missouri were spent trying to keep the boats moving.

The corps tried to keep from getting too much sun. The men also didn't want to get bitten by snakes. There was no way, though, to avoid mosquitoes. The men covered their skin with bear grease. But it didn't keep the mosquitoes away.

In the evenings the corps set up camp, and the cooks made supper. To keep the group happy, one man played the fiddle. Then Lewis and Clark and many of their men wrote down all that they had seen and done that day.

As the corps moved west, it saw animals most people had never seen before. These included bighorn and pronghorn antelope, coyotes, sage grouse, and woodpeckers.

As they moved west, the land around them slowly began to change. There were hardly any trees—just thick green grass that seemed to go on forever. The corps had found the American Great Plains.

With the new land came new plants and animals: buffalo, jackrabbits, antelope, coyotes, prairie dogs, and more. Every day, it seemed, the men saw another creature they had never seen before. Lewis carefully drew and wrote about each one in his journal. Each plant was carefully dried and packed away. If possible, each animal was weighed and measured. Some were even captured to be sent back to President Jefferson.

In the early 1800s most traders used boats like this to travel the Missouri River.

The corps also began to meet Native Americans, including the Missouri, Oto, Sioux, and Arikara. Lewis and Clark always tried to have a friendly meeting with the chiefs. Dressed in formal uniforms, they proudly raised the American flag. They tried to impress the Indians with their sailing equipment and guns. Then they gave them gifts from the United States. Lewis and Clark explained to the Indians that the "great chief of America" had sent the two explorers to make peace. They also said that the United States now claimed the land the native peoples lived on.

Some Native Americans were very friendly. They liked to show off their strength and bravery. Others were more cautious of the explorers. They were used to trading with the French and English and did not want things to change.

The corps stayed in a village for a few days. But as the days grew shorter, the group had to hurry on. The men had hoped to spend the winter at the head of the Missouri. But Lewis soon knew this could not happen. Instead, they would make camp at the last known place on their map. That was near the friendly Mandan and Hidatsa peoples in what is now North Dakota.

Fort Mandan

October 1804–April 1805

By late October the Corps of Discovery had traveled about 1,600 miles (2,574 km). The men were more than happy to spend the winter near the large earth villages of the Mandan and Hidatsa peoples. Both tribes were farming people who were used to trading with white fur trappers. The Mandan called the men in the corps Maci, or "nice people."

The corps spent a month building a fort to live in and called it Fort Mandan. The rest of the winter was spent hunting buffalo and visiting with Indian neighbors. The men wrote in their journals and tried to keep warm in the below-zero weather!

Lewis also used what he knew about medicine to help the villagers. In February he helped one young Indian woman give birth. Her name was Sacagawea. In the fall Lewis had asked her and her husband to join the expedition.

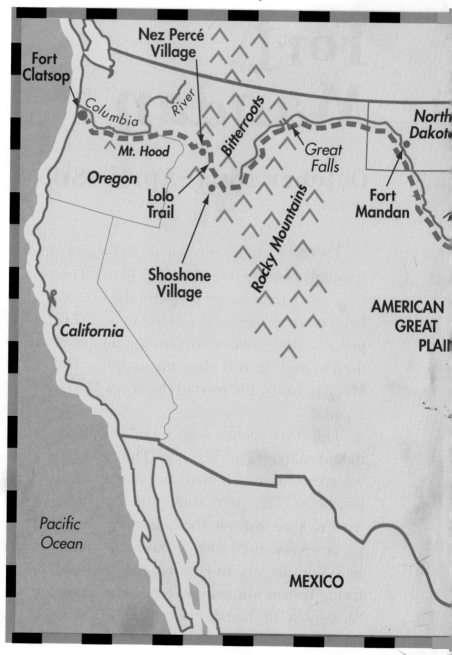

Nez Percé
Village

Fort
Clatsop

Columbia   River

Bitterroots

North
Dakota

Mt. Hood

Great
Falls

Oregon

Lolo
Trail

Fort
Mandan

Rocky Mountains

Shoshone
Village

AMERICAN
GREAT
PLAIN

California

Pacific
Ocean

MEXICO

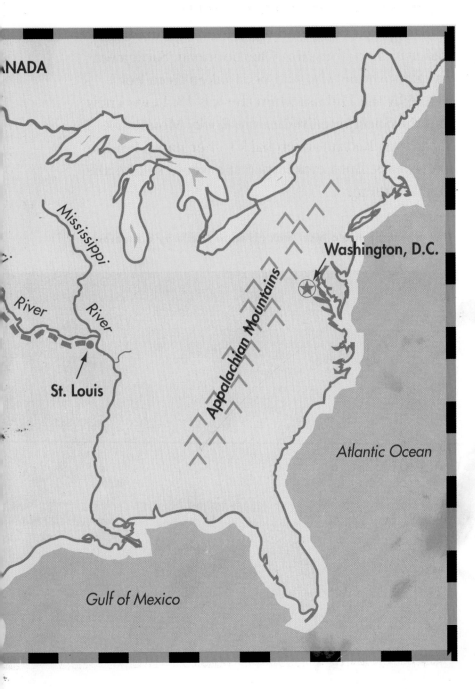

CANADA

Mississippi River

River

St. Louis

Appalachian Mountains

Washington, D.C.

Atlantic Ocean

Gulf of Mexico

Sacagawea's husband was a French Canadian trader named Toussaint Charbonneau. Sacagawea was a Shoshone who had been taken from her village by the Hidatsa when she was 13. Lewis knew that the Shoshone lived in the Rocky Mountains. Sacagawea had not been back to her native lands in many years. But Lewis hoped she would still be able to guide them.

This painted buffalo hide was given to Lewis by a member of the Mandan.

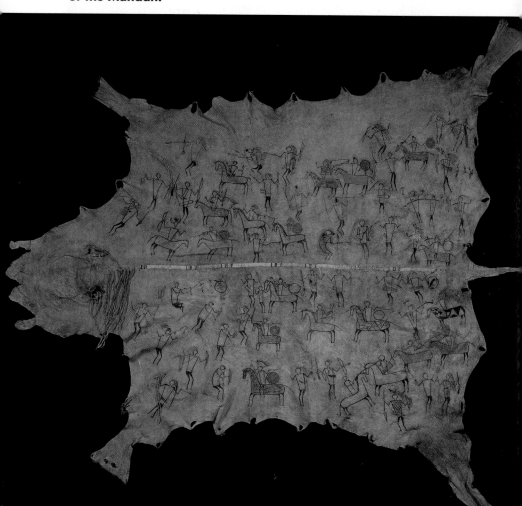

Spring Thaw

April 1805–September 1805

On April 7 Lewis and Clark sent some of the men back down the Missouri. Bound for Washington, D.C., the small group had a boat full of plants and animals they had collected. Then Lewis and Clark set off again. They now had 33 members, including Charbonneau and another French person. Sacagawea and her baby, Jean Baptiste, were with them. They also had a rough map drawn by Clark with the help of the Mandan. The map showed a waterfall and then mountains. Then, Lewis and Clark hoped it would show the Pacific Ocean.

As they paddled up the river in their canoes, the corps seemed happier than ever. Entering what is now Montana, the land became more rugged, but food was not a problem. There were so many buffalo that each man ate nine or ten pounds of meat a day!

The barking of Lewis's dog warned the corps when grizzly bears were near.

This land was also home to grizzly bears. The Mandan had warned Lewis and Clark about these huge, fierce beasts. Still, they were surprised at how savage the grizzlies were—much more so than eastern black bears. Lewis was glad he had brought his dog, Seaman, with him. Many nights the dog would bark and warn the camp when grizzlies came too near.

Near the end of May, Lewis climbed a high bluff on the riverbank. He could see the high mountains that lay before them. "Finally!" he exclaimed, "the Rocky Mountains!" But Lewis was wrong. They were not the Rockies. The Rockies would be even bigger. And they were still 100 miles (160 km) to the west.

Before they reached the mountains, the corps faced other problems. First the men came to a fork in the river that the Mandan and Hidatsa had not told them about. Which way should they go? Most of the men thought they should take the muddy northern fork. But Lewis felt that the southern, clearer fork led to the mountains. He set off on foot to explore it. When he saw the Great Falls ahead of him, he knew he was right. But how would they get over the falls?

They would use portage. This meant they had to carry their boats over land. Clark decided that the only thing to do was build wagons and pull the canoes around the falls. Anything that was too heavy or not needed was hidden or buried. The corps would pick it up on the way home.

The portage was hard work. It took a month to pull the canoes just 18 miles (29 km). By the time the corps passed the falls, it was weeks behind schedule. And the hardest part of the journey still lay ahead.

For the first time in a year, the men were ready to quit. They were weak and sore and tired. Many, as well as Captain Clark, were very sick. They traveled on to the end of the Missouri and finally into the Rocky Mountains.

But as soon as they crossed one mountain, they saw another beyond it. Where was the easy passage they had hoped for? And where were the Shoshone they had hoped would help lead them? Lewis and Clark were worried, but Sacagawea was not. She knew the country. They were near her old Shoshone village, she was sure.

On August 11 Lewis set off on foot with a few men to try to find the village. Two days later he came upon three Shoshone women looking for food. The Shoshone had never seen white men, but Lewis had gifts for them. With sign language he asked the women to take them to their chief.

The Great Falls nearly stopped the corps. They had to pull the boats out of the water and travel by land until they had passed the falls.

The Shoshone did not have much food to trade with the white men. They did, however, have horses that could help the corps cross the mountains. Lewis waited for the rest of the corps to catch up with him. He hoped that Sacagawea would get there soon. She would be able to help him trade with the Shoshone chief.

But when Sacagawea reached the village, she was speechless. She stared at the chief. Then suddenly she ran up to him, threw her blanket around him, and cried. Cameahwait, the Shoshone chief, was Sacagawea's brother!

When the "gates of the mountains" first came into view, Lewis thought the corps had reached the Rocky Mountains. But he was wrong.

Mountains as Far as They Could See

September 1805

It was now September, and Lewis and Clark wanted to keep moving. Clark was feeling better, and both men knew they still had a long way to go. They traded with the Shoshone for horses and a mule and again buried everything they did not need.

Sacagawea's Shoshone family asked her to stay with them. But she said no. She had come this far with Lewis and Clark. She wanted to finish the journey with the rest of the expedition.

Sacagawea was a Shoshone woman. She joined the corps and guided them through the Rocky Mountains.

Facing freezing weather and starvation, Lewis
and Clark separated in the Bitterroot Mountains.

ᏗᏗᎥ

An older Shoshone man they called Old Toby agreed to go with the corps. He had heard of a pass through the mountains called the Lolo Trail. He thought he could help Lewis and Clark find it.

The closer Lewis and Clark got to the large mountains, the more they feared crossing them. For two days they rested their horses and hunted for more food. They also met a small group of Native Americans. They told Lewis and Clark it would take six days to cross the mountains. The next day the corps set off to cross the Bitterroots.

As it turned out, it did not take the corps six days to cross the mountains. It took 11 days. Three days after the men left, a snowstorm hit, and Old Toby lost the trail. Wandering and tired, the corps soon ran out of food. By the time Old Toby found the trail again, several horses had died.

Lewis and Clark were afraid they would freeze or starve. They decided that Clark would go ahead with six men. They would try to find a way out of the Bitterroots. Then they would bring back food for the rest of the corps.

Two days later Clark found a Native American camp at the foot of a mountain. Although they had never seen a white man, the Indians were glad to help the hungry people. Clark sent a man back into the mountains with food for Lewis and the others. Two days after that, members of the corps were together again—happy just to be alive.

Ocean in View

September 1805– November 1805

The natives who fed the starving explorers called themselves the Nimipu, or "Real People." To Clark, however, the sign language symbol for their name looked like a pierced nose. So he called them the "Nez Percé."

The corps stayed with the Nez Percé for two weeks. The men ate bitter roots and salmon. They built new canoes. Lewis and Clark's plan was to return to their water route. They would follow the Clearwater and Snake rivers until they reached the Columbia River. This was the river that would take them to the Pacific. The Nez Percé chief was named Twisted Hair. He agreed to be their guide and interpreter for part of the journey.

Lewis and Clark reach the mouth of the Columbia River.

Traveling with the river's current, the corps traveled farther in a single day than it had in a month. Sometimes, though, the river was too fast. The canoes turned over in the rapids. Supplies were lost. The white water frightened Old Toby so much that he left the expedition. But the corps moved on.

Along the Columbia they reached some very steep waterfalls. The local people gathered by the riverbank to watch the white men risk their lives. But the corps made it through without losing one canoe—or a single member of the party.

In spite of the dangers, the explorers did not slow down. They knew they were close to the end of their journey. They could see a big mountain in the distance. They thought it might be Mount Hood. And they were starting to meet Native Americans who wore sailor caps and spoke English words. This meant that the Indians had met white traders before.

The expedition would never have succeeded without the help of Native Americans.

Then, on November 7, Clark wrote words in his journal that he had been waiting to write for almost two years. "Ocean in view! O! the joy." The corps was very happy. The men forgot about the freezing rain that had been pouring down on them for weeks. They forgot about their dirty clothes and sore bodies. They forgot about everything except getting to that ocean.

Once again Clark was fooled by what he saw. The water ahead of him was not the Pacific—just a very large bay. The corps was still 20 miles (32 km) from the ocean. And the rain was turning to sleet and snow.

In spite of bad weather, the corps traveled on. Seven days later, on November 14, 1805, the first of the group reached the Pacific Ocean. By November 16, they had all arrived at the shore. Tired and chilled from the freezing rain, they were almost too tired to be happy. But the Corps of Discovery had made it to the Pacific Ocean!

A painting by Charles M. Russell shows Native Americans at Ross Hole in the Bitterroot Mountains. This is now part of Montana.

Together the corps decided to make camp on the south side of the Columbia. The native Clatsop people told them they would find plenty of game to hunt and wood for building huts. The corps hurried to build a camp, at Clatsop, before the freezing rain turned into snow.

Homeward Bound

December 1805– September 1806

Lewis and Clark's winter at Fort Clatsop was gloomy. But the men kept busy by preparing for the trip home. They hunted and smoked meat. They made clothes from elk hides, and they made salt by boiling seawater. In his journal Lewis listed all the new plants, animals, and people he had met. Clark used his notes to draw the first map ever made of the land they had seen.

The captains planned to leave Fort Clatsop in April, but by March they were tired of waiting. As soon as the rain stopped and the sun came out, the corps started back up the Columbia River. The explorers traveled the same way they had come.

Lewis and Clark were glad to reach their friend Twisted Hair's village in early June. They tried to cross the Bitterroots right away, but the snow was much too deep. By the time the snow melted, it was nearly July.

Six days later the corps crossed the Lolo Trail into the Bitterroot Valley. Then, for the first time in their journey, Lewis and Clark decided to split up. Although the idea made them nervous, Lewis and Clark knew they could see far more territory this way. Clark would take most of the corps back the way they'd come to the Yellowstone River. He would then explore the Yellowstone all the way to the Missouri. Lewis would take a smaller group and explore a shorter route to the Missouri that the Shoshone had told them about. He would then explore the muddy Marias River, the one his men had once thought was the Missouri.

Six weeks later the two groups met again and traveled on to Fort Mandan. There they said goodbye to Sacagawea and her family. They also said goodbye to one of their men, Private John Colter. Colter liked the West so much he decided to stay there.

Many of the Plains Indians the corps met lived in tepees.

As for the others, the rest of their journey could not go fast enough. Riding the rapid Missouri current, the corps raced down the river. The men cheered when they saw their first cows in more than two years. They were almost home!

Finally, on September 23, Lewis and Clark paddled their canoes into the port of St. Louis. Three shots rang out from the shore in salute. Men, women, and children ran down to greet them. Everyone cheered them. After two years, most Americans had given the group up for dead.

From Sea to Shining Sea

September 1806

Even before his canoe stopped in St. Louis, Lewis began a letter to President Jefferson. "In obedience to your orders," he wrote, "we have penetrated the continent of North America to the Pacific Ocean."

Lewis and Clark were welcomed back as national heroes. There were poems written in their honor and statues carved of them. There were dances and ceremonies for them in big cities as people heard about their success.

40 ⌇⌇

Lewis and Clark admitted that their expedition had not found a true "Northwest Passage." Nor did they find an easy water route from the Missouri to the Pacific. But they had proved that the journey was possible by working together. They also discovered 172 new kinds of plants and 122 new kinds of animals. They made friends with many Native Americans. Most important of all, they answered the question of what the American continent was really like. And they opened it up for generations of Americans to come.

William Clark made treaties with many Native Americans. He also set up Fort Shelby, the first U.S. post in Wisconsin.

Other Events of the 19th Century
(1801 – 1900)

During the century that Lewis and Clark were exploring the American West, events were happening in other parts of the world. Some of these were:

1804	Napoleon Bonaparte proclaims himself emperor of the French.
1807	Inventor Robert Fulton launches his steamboat, the *Clermont*.
1818	Shaka forms Zulu kingdom in southeast Africa.
1822	In Africa, Liberia is founded as a colony for freed slaves.
1823	The German composer Ludwig von Beethoven completes his Ninth Symphony.
1861–1865	The Civil War is fought between the United States and the Confederacy, which is made up of southern states that left the union.
1868	The rule of shoguns (military leaders) ends in Japan.
1869	The Suez Canal opens in Africa.
1876	Alexander Graham Bell invents the telephone.
1879	Mary Cassatt, American-born painter who lived in France, exhibits with the Impressionists in Paris.

Time Line

August 1, 1770   William Clark is born in Caroline County, Virginia.

August 18, 1774   Meriwether Lewis is born in Locust Hill, Virginia.

July 1776   The Declaration of Independence is signed.

1792   American sea captain Robert Gray discovers the Columbia River.

1793   Scotsman Alexander Mackenzie crosses Canada by land.

1801   Thomas Jefferson becomes president of the United States.

1803   The Louisiana Purchase is signed; Jefferson asks Lewis to lead an expedition of discovery.

December 1803   Lewis and Clark build their winter camp, Camp Wood.

May 21, 1804   Corps of Discovery sets off up the Missouri River.

August 3, 1804	Lewis and Clark meet with the Missouri and Oto peoples at Council Bluffs.
August 20, 1804	Sgt. Charles Floyd dies of appendicitis (the only death on the expedition).
August 30, 1804	Lewis and Clark meet with the Yankton Sioux at Calumet Bluff.
September 7, 1804	Lewis and Clark discover prairie dog town.
September 25, 1804	Lewis and Clark meet with Teton Sioux at the Bad River.
October 12, 1804	Lewis and Clark meet with the Arikaras at their village.
October 27, 1804	Corps arrives at Mandan and Hidatsa villages; builds its winter camp, Camp Mandan.
February 11, 1805	Sacagawea gives birth to Jean Baptiste.
April 7, 1805	Corps sets off again up the Missouri.
June 13, 1805	Corps reaches the Great Falls of the Missouri.
June 27, 1805	Corps reaches fork in Missouri.
August 12, 1805	Corps reaches Continental Divide; first shipments of specimens reach Washington, D.C.

September 11, 1805	Corps begins crossing the Bitterroot Mountains along the Lolo Trail.
September 22, 1805	Corps descends from Bitterroots.
October 16, 1805	Corps reaches Columbia River.
November 7, 1805	Clark writes, "Ocean in view!"
November 14–16, 1805	Corps arrives at the Pacific Ocean.
November 24, 1805	Corps votes on where to make winter camp.
December 7, 1805	Winter camp, Fort Clatsop, is completed.
March 23, 1806	Corps begins journey home.
June 24, 1806	Corps follows the Lolo Trail through Bitterroot Mountains.
July 3, 1806	Lewis and Clark split up.
August 12, 1806	Lewis and Clark are reunited.
August 14, 1806	Corps arrives at Mandan and Hidatsa villages.
September 23, 1806	Corps arrives in St. Louis.

Glossary

Bitterroot Mountains (BIT-ter-root mountains) A range of the Rocky Mountains on the border of Idaho and Montana

Columbia River (cuh-LUM-be-uh river) A major river in North America flowing west from Columbia Lake in Canada to the Pacific Ocean

expedition (ek-spuh-DISH-un) A journey for a special purpose, such as to explore

Fort Clatsop (fort CLAT-sop) A fort built by the Lewis and Clark expedition in which to spend the winter of 1805–1806. The fort was located near the village of the Clatsop people, near what is now Astoria, Oregon.

Fort Mandan (fort MAN-dan) A fort built by the Lewis and Clark expedition in which to spend the winter of 1804–1805, located near the village of the Mandan people, near what is now Washburn, North Dakota.

Great Falls A series of mighty waterfalls along the Missouri River in central Montana

keelboat (KEEL boat) A long, shallow riverboat that can be rowed, poled, or towed

Lolo Trail (low-low trail) An Indian trail that the Lewis and Clark expedition followed through the Bitterroot Mountains

Louisiana Purchase (loo-EE-zee-A-nuh PER-chus) About 910,000 sq mi (2,350,000 sq km) between the Mississippi River and the Rocky Mountains bought by the United States from France in 1803

Marias River (muh-RYE-us river) A river flowing from northwest Montana into the Missouri River

Missouri River (muh-ZUR-ee river) Also called "The Big Muddy," a major river in North America flowing east from southwest Montana to the Mississippi River in eastern Missouri

navigation The science of getting from place to place and figuring out position, course, and distance traveled

Northwest Passage A water route across North America that would connect the Atlantic and Pacific oceans

portage (POR-tedge) The act of carrying boats and goods overland, from one body of water to another

Rocky Mountains A major mountain range in North America, running from Alaska to New Mexico

Sacagawea (SACK-uh-juh-WEE-uh) An Indian woman who joined the Lewis and Clark expedition

Yellowstone River (YEL-oh-stone river) A river flowing from northwest Wyoming into eastern Montana and the Missouri River

Index